UNSTOPPABLE
WOMEN WITH DISABILITIES

written by
Helen Wolfe

illustrated by
Karen Patkau

Second Story Press

CONTENTS

I was born with my physical disability. Growing up, I was very lucky. My parents and older sister always encouraged me in everything I wanted to do. I went to elementary school with other kids with disabilities, and then to high school and university with able-bodied students. I worked as a social worker, writer, and teacher for forty years. Through all of those experiences, I hardly saw any people like me and sometimes felt very alone. Imagine how great it would have been to learn about other women with disabilities!

Three women in this book were born with their disabilities. Architect **Karen Braitmayer** uses a wheelchair and brings her personal knowledge and design skills to the work of making buildings accessible and welcoming to everyone. **Maysoon Zayid** has cerebral palsy and looks and moves differently from most people. She is a performer who makes us laugh and shows her audiences what we all have in common. **Karin Muraszko** has worked incredibly hard to become a doctor who operates on her patients' spinal cords and changes their lives.

If you are born able-bodied, suddenly becoming disabled might feel like turning into a different person. **Haben Girma** lost her sight and hearing in childhood, and she is now a lawyer who helps people with disabilities battle discrimination. When she was a child, musician

Christa Couture lost one of her legs and she has suffered many other tragedies. She sings and writes music to cope with life's problems, and proudly shows off her beautiful artificial leg to the world. **Malvika Iyer** lost her hands in an explosion. She makes speeches and uses social media to spread her message of inclusion. Paraplegic **Zhang Haidi** wasn't allowed to attend school and had to study alone to pass her exams, but she was chosen to lead the Chinese Paralympic athletes at the 2022 Games. **Yetnebersh Nigussie** became blind and had to attend a special school for blind kids for the first five years. She eventually earned two university degrees, and created her own school where kids from all different backgrounds study together.

Two women in this book have had to struggle to communicate. After having two strokes, filmmaker **Bonnie Sherr Klein** had to learn to talk all over again. Now, she continues to express her creativity through making films and special art projects. The youngest woman in the book is **Greta Thunberg**, whose autism makes it very hard for her to communicate. Yet, she regularly speaks out on how we need to protect our environment.

You may not have heard of many of these women before. I hope that after you have read *Unstoppable*, you'll feel inspired by their lives and achievements.

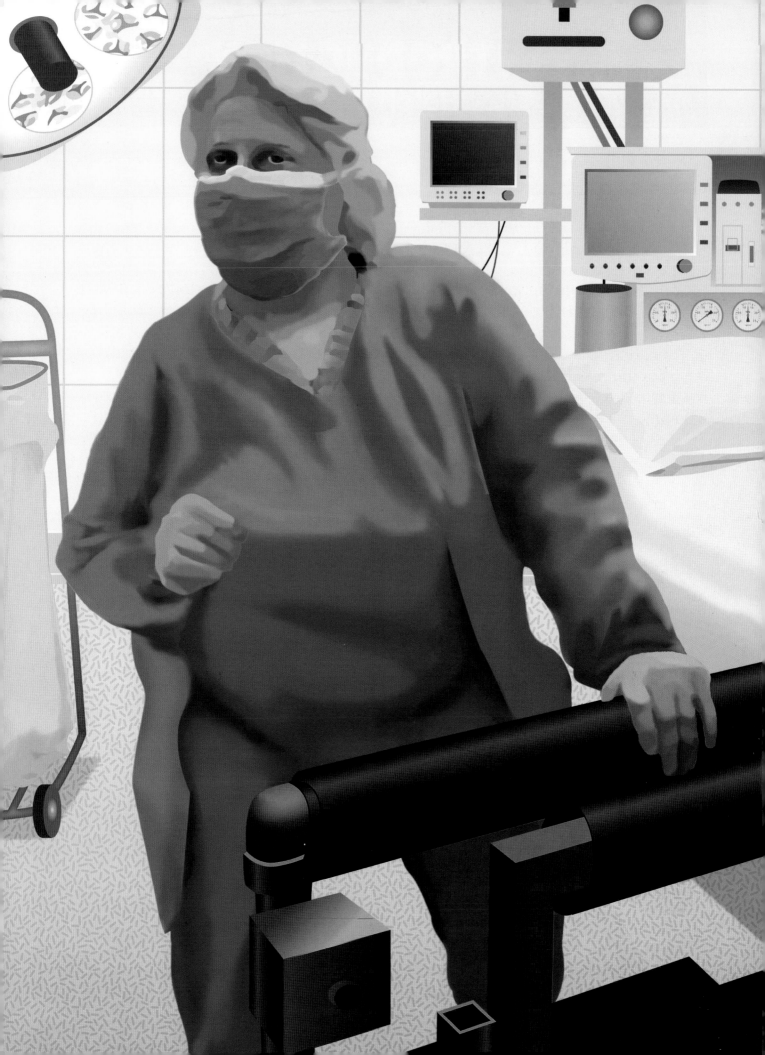

If you ever met Dr. Karin Muraszko, you might not guess what her important job is. Dr. Muraszko is a medical doctor, a surgeon who specializes in performing lifesaving operations. She is also four feet, nine inches tall, and has a disability.

Karin has accomplished many firsts in her life. She was born with a disability called spina bifida. People with spina bifida are often short, and can have difficulty walking and standing. When she was a child, Karin was in a body cast for more than a year and had an operation to shorten one leg to make it the same length as the other one. She really admired the doctors who helped her and decided that she also wanted to be a doctor. At first, she wanted to study to be a psychiatrist, treating people who have emotional problems. She thought it would be the most practical kind of medicine for someone with a physical disability.

But in her third year, she watched an operation on a man who was losing the ability to use his arms and hands. The surgeon operated on his patient's spinal cord, and Karin saw that the doctor's skill restored the patient's use of his hands. She realized then that neurosurgery was her dream. After medical school, Karin earned a seven-year residency at Columbia University in New York City, becoming the first person with a disability to be offered that position. Although some surgeons doubted that Karin could do a physically demanding job, she proved them wrong. Besides operating on patients, Karin has also taught and trained doctors who have become famous neurosurgeons. One of them is Dr. Sanjay Gupta, chief medical correspondent on the CNN television network. In 2016, Dr. Gupta paid Karin a great compliment by including her in the CNN documentary *The Person Who Changed My Life.* Since 2005, Karin has been the head of neurosurgery at the University of Michigan, and is the first woman in the United States to have that job.

As a surgeon, Karin's focus is operating on young children and teenagers, who hold a special place in her heart because of her own childhood experiences with surgery. Karin's words reveal her compassion and strength:

"When I look at those kids...what I want to say to them is just, 'Hold on. Hold on until you get to be eighteen or nineteen, and everybody around you gets more mature, and you're going to find out that everybody's different.'"

BONNIE SHERR KLEIN
Changing Our Ideas about Disability

When you are born with a disability or become disabled as a child, learning to cope becomes part of life. However, anyone who becomes disabled as an adult asks many questions that a child wouldn't ask. For example, will I still be able to do my job? Will my friends still want to spend time with me?

Bonnie Sherr Klein is an American director, producer, and author who moved to Canada in the early 1980s to make films. She worked hard to create movies about social problems and became famous for one called *Not a Love Story*.

Bonnie's life changed forever when she had two strokes. A stroke is a sudden injury to the brain, which controls many parts of our bodies. After having a stroke, people often have difficulty speaking, and moving one or both sides of their body. Speech and physical therapy can help a lot, but stroke survivors sometimes have to deal with these changes for the rest of their lives.

Most people who have strokes are senior citizens, but Bonnie was only forty-six years old. For a while, she experienced "locked-in syndrome." She understood everything happening around her but couldn't speak or move. For the next several years, she had to have special therapy to learn to speak again and to move her body. This therapy included special exercises to improve her movement in her arms and legs. She also needed to relearn how to do everyday tasks, such as dressing herself, cooking, and cleaning.

After her recovery, Bonnie decided to focus her work on what it was like to have a stroke. In 1997, she wrote *Slow Dance: A Story of Stroke, Love and Disability*, which tells the story of her discovering new ways to live. She also helped to organize KickstART!, a festival celebrating arts and culture created by people with disabilities. In 2006, Bonnie made the film *Shameless: The ART of Disability*, which looks at the lives of five disabled artists. In her film, she shows that people with disabilities are energetic artists who contribute their gifts to society.

Now Bonnie wants to motivate other filmmakers with disabilities to follow her lead and carry on where she has left off.

"To other filmmakers with disabilities, I say, 'Do it!' There are opportunities and there are challenges, and there are many more films to be made. We have our own stories and people are hungry."

Do you love to sing or play a musical instrument? Does singing and playing music help you to express both happy and sad feelings, and to cope with them better?

Canadian singer-songwriter Christa Couture has had to deal with many hardships. She is mixed Cree and Scandinavian, and her ancestors were among Canada's First Nations. Christa grew up in a very musical household. Her father performed Cree ceremonial music, while her mother sang Canadian folk music in a small group. Music was always used to teach, to express love, and helped her to remember important ideas.

When she was only eleven years old, Christa's life changed forever because she was diagnosed with bone cancer, and had to have her leg amputated to save her life. Losing her leg affected Christa's self-esteem. But gradually, she learned to adapt and became a well-known singer. Christa's fans went online to raise $25,000 for a new prosthetic leg. She had it decorated with a floral design, which looks like a beautiful tattoo.

Christa is a songwriter who uses music to deal with life's tragedies. Sadly, she had two sons who died when they were babies. Around the same time, Christa also divorced her husband. She wrote and performed music to cope with these losses.

Christa has written and produced several music albums and has also found other ways to share her thoughts. For example, she has written essays about grief, disability, and other problems faced by women. In the middle of her busy life, Christa also made the very important decision to come out as a lesbian.

Finally, she gave birth to a healthy baby girl. When she was pregnant, she wrote an article about becoming a mother and was bravely photographed without her prosthetic leg. She also hosts a radio show where she plays music and speaks out about issues that are important to women and people with disabilities. In late 2020, Christa's new book, *How to Lose Everything*, was published.

Despite facing so many life challenges, Christa Couture is a fearless and gifted artist. Christa's beliefs about using music to deal with feelings are summarized by her own words:

"Grief is a very lonely feeling, and so getting to make songs about it and share those songs was a way that I could be less alone."

HABEN GIRMA
Opening the World to Deaf-Blind People

American Haben Girma, who is both deaf and blind, not only deals with her own disabilities, but is also dedicated to helping those with the same challenges. Haben's parents emigrated from Eritrea. Haben was born in California, and lost both her sight and hearing because of a family illness.

Growing up, Haben benefited from a law called the Americans with Disabilities Act (ADA), which says that all people with disabilities must have the same rights to education and jobs as all other Americans. She mastered accessible computer technology, such as a digital braille device, which helped her become an excellent student.

Haben is also someone who is eager to help others. After graduating high school, she attended college and saw that students with disabilities were not able to use the school cafeteria. So, she led a successful campaign to make it accessible.

After graduating college, Haben decided to become a lawyer. Always ready for a challenge, she attended Harvard Law School, one of the hardest law schools in the United States to get into, and graduated in 2013.

Haben believes that having equal access to education is the key to having your best life. She wants to change attitudes about people with disabilities and to develop accessible computers and digital services.

In 2014, Haben represented the American National Federation of the Blind in a lawsuit against a company that didn't provide accessible reading material to blind readers. She won the case, and that company must now provide appropriate reading materials to everyone.

Haben also gave a TEDx talk in Baltimore, Maryland, where she courageously criticized the organizers for not providing captions of their talks for their deaf audience.

On July 20, 2015, for the 25th anniversary of the Americans with Disabilities Act, she spoke in front of then-President Barack Obama about the importance of accessible technology for people with disabilities, and explained her philosophy for success:

"We know that people with disabilities succeed not by magic, but from the opportunities afforded by America and the hard-won power of the ADA."

Do you know what it means when a building is "wheelchair accessible?" A building is wheelchair accessible when it has ramps, elevators, and special washrooms that people with physical challenges need. Canada, the United States, and many other countries have laws requiring new buildings to be accessible. Karen Braitmayer, from Seattle, Washington, completely understands wheelchair accessibility. Karen was born with osteogenesis imperfecta, also called brittle bone disease, and has always used a wheelchair.

At school, she had all her classes with able-bodied classmates and wasn't treated any differently from them.

Her grades four, five, and six classrooms were on the school's second floor, so either her mother or one of the school staff would carry her up and down the stairs every day. Because her mother and the school staff did that, Karen was able to go to school with all of her classmates. When she was sixteen, one of Karen's teachers even taught her how to drive a hand-controlled car, which made her very independent.

After earning a Bachelor's degree at university, Karen worked for a while, and then she returned to school to earn a Master's degree in architecture. An architect designs buildings, which can be private homes or public spaces. While she was working in an architectural company, Karen noticed that some buildings her co-workers designed didn't include ramps, special elevators, or accessible washrooms.

Eventually, Karen decided to open her own company, Studio Pacifica, and advise other architects on making their buildings accessible. Karen consulted on renovating one of Seattle, Washington's most famous landmarks, The Space Needle. It was originally built in 1962, when people really didn't understand wheelchair accessibility. Also, it wasn't until thirty years later that the American government passed laws which made it illegal for buildings to be inaccessible. Able-bodied visitors could stand on the observation deck and look out at a breathtaking view of the city. But people using wheelchairs, or with other disabilities preventing them from seeing over the railing, didn't have the same view. So, Karen designed glass elevators and huge windows. Now, everyone can enjoy these spectacular views.

Karen Braitmayer is a gifted architect who loves her work and is committed to creating accessible, inclusive public spaces.

"Good design does have to be thoughtful. Good design lets you in the door and makes you welcome to sit down."

People who can use their hands to do all their everyday tasks don't think about it very much. How many times do we use them to pick up, carry, and touch objects and people every single day?

Until she was thirteen, Malvika Iyer had an ideal childhood in her hometown of Bikaner, India. But on May 26, 2002, her life changed forever. Malvika picked up an object in her garage, not realizing that it was a live grenade, which then exploded. This terrible accident left her without her hands and her legs very badly injured.

Because she needed so much physical therapy, Malvika missed the rest of grade nine and all of grade ten. At the end of grade ten, Indian students take government exams. With only three months to prepare, Malvika focused on doing well. Because she didn't have hands, she got special permission to dictate her exam answers to someone who could write answers for her. Malvika scored 483 out of a perfect score of 500. Her accomplishment impressed everyone so much that she was invited to meet Dr. A.P.J. Abdul Kalam, then-president of India.

Malvika studied economics and social work in university, but was still worried about other people's opinion of her. While she was studying social work, she was inspired by the positive attitudes of the children with disabilities she worked with.

Malvika spreads her message of inclusion as a motivational speaker in many countries. She also tells leaders in those countries that all buildings must be accessible for people with disabilities.

This modern young woman uses technology and social media campaigns to show positive images of people with disabilities. She also believes that it's very important to design fashionable and easy-to-wear clothing for people with disabilities. She received the first Women in the World Emerging Leaders Award in 2016 and also acted in a short film about inclusion called *The Phoenix*.

Malvika calmly deals with life's problems. For example, if it's too hot and her prosthetic hands slip off, she puts them back on and keeps going. Her determination and positive philosophy can be summed up by these words:

"Now I concentrate on my own abilities and not on people's reactions towards me. That's all it took to change my life."

You've probably seen people with disabilities going to school and playing sports. Countries such as the United States and Canada have accessible facilities, which allow everyone to participate in daily life.

In China, about twenty-six million people have some kind of disability, and Zhang Haidi is one of them. At the age of five, Zhang lost the use of her legs. She had several operations, which made her disability even worse, and eventually she couldn't walk at all. Zhang's mother carried her to school on her back, but they were told that the school didn't enroll "crippled children." So, for ten years, Zhang stayed at home in bed. This was about fifty years ago. Email and social media didn't exist, and there was no way for her to make friends.

Since she wasn't allowed to go to school, Zhang decided she would teach herself subjects such as math, science, history, and geography. She also learned to speak, read, and write in English, Japanese, and German. After studying alone for ten years, Zhang took high-school graduation exams and qualified to enter university, eventually earning a Master's degree in philosophy and starting work as a translator.

In 1983, a newspaper wrote an article about Zhang, which made her famous. The Chinese government was so impressed that she had taught herself that they asked her to tour the country, giving speeches to motivate young people.

As a child, Zhang expressed her loneliness in a diary. When she grew up, she used these memories to write a novel, *Dreams in a Wheelchair*, which has also been made into a movie.

Zhang encourages the government, schools, and private businesses to improve opportunities for people with disabilities. She was elected the chairperson of China's Disabled Person's Federation and speaks about providing more exercise programs. The Chinese government is listening and creating programs to help its many disabled citizens.

The 2022 Winter Paralympics, an athletic competition for athletes with physical challenges, will be in Beijing, China. Zhang will be the head organizer of the Chinese Paralympians. She feels it's very important for China to show it respects and cares about athletes who are able-bodied and those with disabilities.

"A lot of brothers and sisters will come to China to train for the games. The whole nation will make a great endeavor to make the Winter Olympics and Paralympics a success and help people with disabilities to live better lives."

YETNEBERSH NIGUSSIE
Making Ethiopia More Accessible

In many countries, people with disabilities attend college or university to study for their careers. The laws in these countries have guaranteed that everyone has equal opportunity for education. Unfortunately, people with disabilities in some countries do not have the same rights.

At five years old, Yetnebersh Nigussie from Ethiopia had an illness called meningitis, which left her blind, and she went to a special school for blind children. When she was twelve, her parents decided that she was ready to attend a school where all the other students could see.

She was very lonely. Students at her new school had never seen or been friends with a blind person before. But smart Yetnebersh became popular because she helped other kids with their schoolwork. In secondary school, she was the leader of the student council.

She attended university in her country's capital city and earned degrees in law and social work. She also became a leader in organizations helping people with disabilities. In 2005, she co-founded the Ethiopian Center for Disability and Development (ECDD), which encourages disabled and able-bodied people to work together. They advise government and businesses about making workplaces more friendly to women and to people with disabilities. Yetnebersh has been using this center to help women and people with disabilities begin to earn their own living and become more independent.

The ECDD has also identified a list of office buildings, hotels, and restaurants that are accessible to people with disabilities. Yetnebersh advises the government on laws ensuring that any new buildings will be accessible. She has started the Yetnebersh Modern Academy, a school where 190 able-bodied and disabled girls and boys from poorer families study together.

In 2017, at age thirty, Yetnebersh received the Swedish Right Livelihood Award for her work. The award is given to people who have spent their lives doing important work for others, and Yetnebersh was very young to receive it.

Yetnebersh works to improve the lives of women and people with disabilities in Ethiopia and all over the world. The hopefulness and determination that she has shown in her own life are qualities that she is using to improve lives everywhere. She isn't focused on what a person cannot do, but on the strengths that we all possess.

"Focus on the person, not the disability. We have one disability, but ninety-nine abilities to build on."

MAYSOON ZAYID
Using Humor to Deal with Challenges

When she was a child, Maysoon Zayid dreamed of becoming a famous actress. But, for her, that goal would be harder to achieve. She was born with cerebral palsy. Often, her arms and legs don't move smoothly, and she shakes all the time.

Maysoon's parents are Palestinian, but she was born in New Jersey. Maysoon was lucky because her parents didn't treat her any differently from her sisters. Her father taught her to walk by having her stand on his feet. And instead of having physical therapy like a lot of people with disabilities, Maysoon's parents gave her the same dance and piano lessons that her sisters had.

Maysoon studied acting at university. But, because of her disability and her culture, an acting teacher told her that she would never work. Determined to become an entertainer, she took stand-up comedy classes instead. Today, Maysoon uses humor to teach people about her disability and her culture and has made her living by performing in comedy clubs, telling jokes and funny stories about her life and family.

On September 11, 2001, there were terrible terrorist attacks in New York City, Washington, and Pennsylvania, which killed almost three thousand people. Some people, including some Americans, blamed all Muslim people, saying they were all terrorists, and bullied them about their clothing, traditions, and religion. Maysoon, who is a Muslim, believed that she needed to use humor to show that Muslim people are just like everyone else. So, she created the New York Arab-American Comedy Festival, where Arab-American comedians get to show off their talents.

Maysoon feels a responsibility to pass on her message of acceptance. She is the first woman comedian ever to perform in Palestine and Jordan. She created Maysoon's Kids, a charity that works with children living in refugee camps who are growing up in the middle of gunfire and enemy raids. She also runs welfare programs and training sessions for parents and teachers of children who became disabled because of war injuries.

Maysoon displays her optimistic approach to life in her very popular TED Talk. Negative images of people with disabilities and Muslims have no place in her life.

As she says, she wants to be "the image of the American you don't think is American."

Greta Thunberg from Sweden is a world-famous climate change activist. When she was eight, Greta first became angry that adults—who were supposed to take care of important problems—didn't take the threats to the environment seriously. So, she decided to make her own changes. She promised not to fly in airplanes, eat meat or dairy foods, or to buy anything new that she didn't need.

Greta was diagnosed with Autism Spectrum Disorder, which makes it hard for her to communicate. She also has "selective mutism," and only speaks when necessary. Greta sees these challenges as giving her a kind of "superpower." Someone with selective mutism is very anxious when they speak in public. So, when Greta does speak, this courageous young woman knows it's important.

To reduce their carbon footprint, Greta challenged her parents to stop eating meat, to recycle more, and to give up flying too, telling them that if they didn't do these things, they would be "stealing her future." Greta's mother even gave up her career as an opera singer because of her promise not to fly.

In August 2018, Greta joined the movement to prevent climate change. Some young people had organized "school strikes." But, she didn't think action was moving fast enough. So,

Greta decided to strike by herself and stayed away for the first three weeks of the school year. She stood alone outside the Swedish parliament trying to force the government to reduce carbon emissions.

In 2019, Greta was the youngest person ever to receive the Swedish Right Livelihood Award, for people who offer practical answers to human challenges.

Greta also uses social media to spread her message. She uses Instagram and Twitter to get worldwide attention, and her speech at the United Nations Climate Action Summit went viral. In that speech, Greta courageously said this to world leaders:

"You have stolen my dreams and my childhood with your empty words…. People are suffering. People are dying…. We are in the beginning of a mass extinction…. How dare you?"

Climate change isn't the only cause Greta is fighting for. Since late 2019, the Covid-19 virus pandemic has killed millions of people. Greta gave a $100,000 grant she got for climate activism to fight the virus. In May 2020, she posted a powerful message on her Instagram account asking kids to wear masks, keep a social distance from their friends, and pledged to raise more money to help victims during the pandemic.

ABOUT THE AUTHOR

Helen Wolfe's career has spanned over forty years in publishing, social work, and education. Her extensive teaching experience was in special education, history, English, guidance, and English as a Second Language (ESL). For almost thirty years, her work focused on helping ESL adults to achieve their potential. Helen has also authored over thirty teacher's guides to accompany books and a documentary for students of all levels and ages, with a particular focus on Holocaust literature and education. In 2011, Second Story Press published her first non-fiction chapter book for young readers, entitled *Terrific Women Teachers*.

ABOUT THE ILLUSTRATOR

Karen Patkau graduated from the University of Manitoba with a Bachelor of Fine Arts Honours degree, and became interested in visual storytelling while studying for her Master of Visual Arts degree at the University of Alberta. She has been writing and illustrating for many years. Her work appears in children's picture books, educational publications, posters, advertisements, magazines, package designs, greeting cards, and art exhibitions. Karen also has a lifelong disability and walks with a prosthetic leg. Karen lives in Toronto.

This book is dedicated to my parents, Toby and Joseph Wolfe, who always encouraged me to strive for and achieve new goals, and to my sister, Margie Wolfe, who has given me this opportunity to write about the extraordinary women in this book.
—Helen Wolfe

To my parents and to Sylvia, my unstoppable friend.
—Karen Patkau

Acknowledgments:
I would like to express my heartfelt gratitude to the staff of Second Story Press for their invaluable support in writing this book. My special thanks go out to Gillian Rodgerson and Jordan Ryder for their thoughtful and intelligent editorial input, and to Melissa Kaita for her hard work on the production of *Unstoppable*. **—H.W.**

LIBRARY AND ARCHIVES CANADA CATALOGUING IN PUBLICATION

Title: Unstoppable : women with disabilities / written by Helen Wolfe ; illustrated by Karen Patkau.
Names: Wolfe, Helen, 1953- author. | Patkau, Karen, illustrator.
Identifiers: Canadiana 20210135891 | ISBN 9781772602098 (hardcover)
Subjects: LCSH: Women with disabilities—Biography—Juvenile literature. | LCSH: Women with disabilities—Juvenile literature. | LCGFT: Biographies.
Classification: LCC HV1569.3.W65 W64 2021 | DDC j362.4082—dc23

Printed and bound in China

Second Story Press gratefully acknowledges the support of the Ontario Arts Council, the Ontario Media Development Corporation, and the Canada Council for the Arts for our publishing program. We acknowledge the financial support of the Government of Canada through the Canada Book Fund.

ONTARIO ARTS COUNCIL
CONSEIL DES ARTS DE L'ONTARIO
an Ontario government agency
un organisme du gouvernement de l'Ontario

Canada Council
for the Arts
Conseil des arts
du Canada

Funded by the Government of Canada
Financé par le gouvernement du Canada | Canada

Published by
Second Story Press
20 Maud Street, Suite 401
Toronto, ON
M5V 2M5
www.secondstorypress.ca